GODDESSES OF INDIA

Shachi the Consort of Indra

SHUBHA VILAS

Om KIDZ
An imprint of Om Books International

Shachi or Indrani, the consort of Lord Indra was beautiful, virtuous and pure. She is worshipped as one of the seven divine mother goddesses. A puja dedicated exclusively to Goddess Indrani is performed during the Ashada Navratri time as she is believed to bless devotees with welfare and good life. Lord Indra had blessed her with immortality.

Once, Indra had to fight a battle against Vritra who was an extremely powerful brahmin who was also a demon. Realising that he might lose, Indra went to Vishnu for help.

Vishnu advised him to make a weapon from Dadhichi Muni's bones and use that to kill Vritrasura. Dadhichi Muni happily sacrificed himself to donate his bones to Indra. Indra then used his powerful weapon to kill Vritrasura.

However, after killing Vritra, Indra wanted to repent for his sin of killing a brahmin and he disappeared from his heavenly home. The devatas had to find a replacement for him. They chose Nahusha, who had performed a hundred Ashwamedha yajnas. His name and fame had already reached heaven.

Nahusha soon became proud and arrogant. He began to inflict atrocities on his people. One day, he chanced upon Shachi, the beautiful wife of Indra. Everything that once belonged to Indra was his, then why not his wife too? Without any shame, he proposed to Shachi, 'Will you marry me, my beautiful lady?'

Shachi was aghast and left the palace. She headed straight to meet their guru, Brihaspati. Only he could show her and the devatas a way to deal with this proud man.

Brihaspati outlined his plan to Shachi and she agreed to it. As per the plan, she sent a message to Nahusha through Agni that she was ready to accept his proposal. But the condition was that he should come after fifteen days in a palanquin carried by the eight greatest sages of the world.

Shachi used those fifteen days to find the whereabouts of Indra. And where did she find him? Meditating inside a lotus, under water, atoning for his sin of killing Vritrasura.

When Indra heard the horrors of what his people had to suffer, he was devastated. How could he not come back now knowing that heaven was in danger?

Meanwhile, fifteen days had passed and Nahusha was gearing up to marry Shachi. He had assembled the greatest sages to carry the palanquin, not knowing that these sages were the most powerful people in the world, more powerful than him.

He was in such a hurry to meet his beloved that he kicked sage Agastya to make him walk faster.

'Sarpa, sarpa,' he screamed at the sage, ordering him to move faster.

Sage Agastya was aghast at this outrageous behaviour and out came a curse from his mouth. 'Become a sarpa (snake). This is what you deserve to be.'

At that very moment, the cruel King Nahusha transformed into a huge python! As he fell on Earth, he quietly glided away, sad and forlorn.

Shachi and Indra happily became king and queen of heaven and the world was restored to normalcy.